W9-CNR-096

Young Naturalist
Field Guides

Snakes, Salamanders, and Lizards

by Diane L. Burns

illustrations by Linda Garrow

Gareth Stevens Publishing
MILWAUKEE

DEDICATION

For today's children, who are tomorrow's herpetologists.
Save room in your world for untamed creatures.

ACKNOWLEDGMENTS

Grateful thanks to my brother, and sister-in-law, Jim and Kirsten,
who generously emptied their library on behalf of my research
and answered countless questions. Also, my husband, Phil, for additional
herpetological knowledge and especially for ongoing support and patience.

**For a free color catalog describing Gareth Stevens' list of high-quality books
and multimedia programs, call 1-800-542-2595 (USA) or 1-800-461-9120 (Canada).
Gareth Stevens Publishing's Fax: (414) 225-0377.
See our catalog, too, on the World Wide Web: http://gsinc.com**

Library of Congress Cataloging-in-Publication Data

Burns, Diane L.
    Snakes, salamanders, and lizards / by Diane L. Burns; illustrated by Linda
Garrow.
        p.   cm. — (Young naturalist field guides)
    Originally published: Minocqua, Wis. : NorthWord Press, Inc., © 1995, in
series: Take-along guide. With new index.
    Includes bibliographical references and index.
    Summary: A field guide introducing thirty species of snakes, salamanders,
and lizards.
    ISBN 0-8368-2042-8 (lib. bdg.)
    1. Snakes—Juvenile literature. 2. Salamanders—Juvenile literature.
3. Lizards—Juvenile literature. [1. Snakes. 2. Salamanders. 3. Lizards.]
I. Garrow, Linda, ill. II. Title. III. Series.
QL666.O6B887   1998
597.9—dc21   97-31857

This North American edition first published in 1998 by
Gareth Stevens Publishing
1555 North RiverCenter Drive, Suite 201
Milwaukee, Wisconsin 53212 USA

Based on the book, *Snakes, Salamanders and Lizards*, written by Diane L. Burns, first
published in the United States in 1995 by NorthWord Press, Inc., Minocqua, Wisconsin.
© 1995 by Diane L. Burns. Illustrations by Linda Garrow. Book design by Lisa Moore.
Additional end matter © 1998 by Gareth Stevens, Inc.

Printed in Mexico

1 2 3 4 5 6 7 8 9 02 01 00 99 98

CONTENTS
Snakes, Salamanders and Lizards

Metric Conversion Table

mm = millimeter = 0.0394 inch
cm = centimeter = 0.394 inch
m = meter = 3.281 feet

Note: Metric equivalents below are rounded off.

0.25 inch = 0.63 cm (6.3 mm)	5 feet = 1.5 m
1 inch = 2.5 cm (25 mm)	10 feet = 3 m
10 inches = 25 cm	15 feet = 4.6 m
12 inches (1 foot) = 30 cm	25 feet = 7.6 m
1 foot = 0.3 m	100 feet = 30 m
3 feet = 0.9 m	300 feet = 91 m

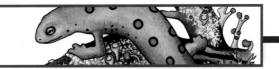

SNAKES

Snakes are animals known as reptiles. Reptiles have skin made up of scales.

They are cold-blooded. The air temperature decides their body temperature. If the air is too cold or too warm, the snake will die.

Snakes have scales that are clean and dry. The skin does not stretch as the snake grows. The snake must shed its skin at least once a year.

Snakes hibernate in cold weather. They have no arms or legs. Snakes use small, hooked teeth to grab and hold their food.

Each side of a snake's lower jaw moves. This lets the snake eat food bigger than its mouth.

Snakes sense odors with their tongues.

There are about 115 different kinds of snakes in the United States.

Most snakes are harmless. Some are poisonous.

Most snakes squeeze their prey to death and swallow it whole. Poisonous snakes use their venom to kill prey.

Tell an adult where you are going or take one with you.

COMMON GARTER SNAKE

Tips to find this snake

Garter snakes are usually found in fields or grassy woods.

On warm days, they rest in sunny spots.

Garter snakes are active during the day.

WHAT IT LOOKS LIKE

In the East, garter snakes have yellow stripes on their dark bodies. In the West, both the stripes and their bodies may be red-orange. Sometimes their heads are red. The stripes on all garter snakes run the length of their bodies.

They grow to be 4 feet long. Garter snakes are pencil-thin and look fragile.

WHAT IT EATS

Garter snakes eat earthworms, slugs, birds, grasshoppers, and small rodents like mice.

WHERE IT LIVES

Garter snakes are found everywhere in the United States except for the southwestern deserts.

INTERESTING FACTS

The garter snake is named for old-fashioned garters, which men once used to hold up their socks.

SPECIAL WARNING

They will bite if threatened. Be careful!

5

GREEN SNAKE

Tips to find this snake

Green snakes are active during the day.

On warm days, they may be found in meadows and pastures.

They also live close to the ground near ponds and streams.

WHAT IT LOOKS LIKE

These snakes are hard to see. Whether lying still or zipping away, they blend in. Their bodies are bright green on top. They are pale yellow-white on their bellies.

Green snakes are slender, and about 2 feet long.

WHAT IT EATS

Green snakes eat spiders, caterpillars, and grasshoppers.

WHERE IT LIVES

Green snakes are found in the northeastern and central United States and south to Florida and the Gulf Coast into Texas.

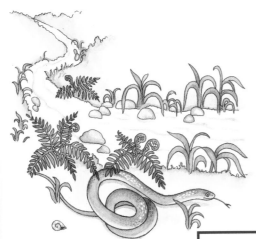

Get permission before going onto someone's land.

WATER SNAKE

Water snakes have as many as 100 babies at a time.

Tips to find this snake

During warm spring and summer days, water snakes rest in the sun.

Look for water snakes on logs, or on branches hanging over water.

Water snakes like ditches, canals, marshes, ponds, bayous, and lakes.

WHAT IT LOOKS LIKE

Their bodies are usually solid brown on top, but they can also be grayish or blue-black. Some have light and dark brown diamond shapes on them.

Sometimes there are dark brown crossbands on its body or belly. The water snake's belly is likely to be either red or yellow.

They are thin snakes that grow to be 2 to 3 feet long.

WHAT IT EATS

Water snakes eat small fish and frogs.

WHERE IT LIVES

Water snakes are found in the Mississippi River valley and the Great Lakes region. They also live in the south-eastern United States west into Texas, Oklahoma, and Kansas.

SPECIAL WARNING

Don't touch! They will bite. Wear boots!

7

KINGSNAKE

Tips to find this snake

Kingsnakes are most active in early morning or early evening, especially in hot weather.

Sometimes they hide under rocks.

The harmless eastern milk snake (which is a kind of kingsnake) looks like the poisonous copperhead.

Kingsnakes often look like the deadly coral snake. Here is a good rhyme to remember how to tell them apart:

"Red touch yellow, kill a fellow. Red touch black, venom lack."

That means if a red stripe is touching a yellow stripe, the snake is a dangerous coral snake. And you should stay away.

WHAT IT LOOKS LIKE

Kingsnakes can be black, brown, or red. They have blotches or bands or speckles.

Kingsnakes have thick bodies and grow from 3 to 6 feet long.

WHAT IT EATS

Kingsnakes find birds, lizards, and rodents to be tasty treats.

WHERE IT LIVES

Kingsnakes are found throughout the United States, in swamps, forests, plains, deserts, and mountains.

SPECIAL WARNING

Don't touch or approach!

RATTLESNAKE

Tips to find this snake

Rattlesnakes are active at night.

During the day, they rest in the shade of rocks and logs.

You can see them only from May through September. They hibernate during the other months.

WHAT IT LOOKS LIKE

The body of a rattler is brown-gray, and it is thick and solid. Dark blotches or diamond shapes along the back and sides of its body are usually edged in dark brown.

The rattlesnake grows from 4 to 8 feet long.

WHAT IT EATS

Rattlers eat small rodents such as mice, and birds that like to stay close to the ground.

WHERE IT LIVES

Some types of rattlesnakes live east of the Mississippi River. They like forests and rocky highlands. Some also live in swampy areas.

Rattlesnakes west of the Mississippi live in the deserts and mountains. They also like dry, rocky buttes.

INTERESTING FACTS

The rattlesnake's teeth, called fangs, are hollow.

The fangs are also moveable. They lay against the roof of the snake's mouth when they are not being used.

The rattling noise is made by hard, horn-like buttons at the tip of the tail. A button is added there every time the snake sheds its skin.

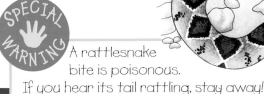

SPECIAL WARNING

A rattlesnake bite is poisonous. If you hear its tail rattling, stay away!

9

COPPERHEAD

WHAT IT LOOKS LIKE

Copperheads have thick bodies the color of toasted marshmallows. On its back and sides are red-brown hourglass-shaped blotches.

Copperheads grow to be 2 to 3 feet long.

WHAT IT EATS

Copperheads eat mice, rabbits, lizards, and frogs.

WHERE IT LIVES

Copperheads are found from Massachusetts south to Georgia and west as far as Kansas and Texas.

Tips to find this snake

Copperheads are usually active during the day. But, during very hot weather they are active at night.

In spring and fall, copperheads are found around rocks and in dry, deep woods.

In summer, copperheads like cool and wet areas.

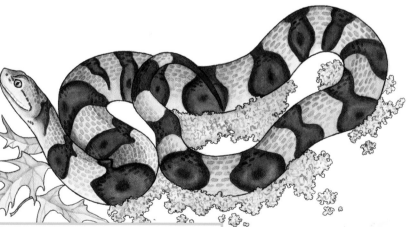

SPECIAL WARNING

The copperhead's bite is poisonous!
Do not approach!

HOGNOSE SNAKE

Tips to find this snake

Hognose snakes like dry sandy places, like open woods and fields or sandpits.

Look for them in areas that have dead leaves on the ground, too.

SPECIAL NOTE
A hognose may try to scare you by hissing and puffing out its head. Don't tease it.

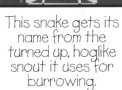

INTERESTING FACTS

This snake gets its name from the turned up, hoglike snout it uses for burrowing.

When threatened, a hognose may flop over and "play dead!"

WHAT IT LOOKS LIKE

Sometimes their body color is solid. It can be gray, green, rusty red, or brown. Hognoses sometimes have blotchy patterns on their backs in gray, brown, or black. The belly color is usually lighter than the body color.

They have thick bodies and grow to be 2 to 4 feet long.

WHAT IT EATS

Hognoses eat toads, mice, and birds.

WHERE IT LIVES

Hognose snakes are found everywhere in the United States except in the western mountains and deserts.

SPECIAL WARNING

Sometimes, they bite. Don't touch! Their saliva is not poisonous, but it can be harmful.

BULLSNAKE

INTERESTING FACTS

This snake gets its name from its hiss, which sounds like a grunting bull.

Bullsnakes eat rats and mice in barns and sheds, so farmers and ranchers like them.

Tips to find this snake

Bullsnakes are active during the day.

Besides farmland, they like sandy pine woods and prairies.

WHAT IT LOOKS LIKE

Its yellow-tan body has large, red-brown blotches along the back and sides.

Bullsnakes have heavy, solid bodies and grow to be about 10 feet long.

WHAT IT EATS

Bullsnakes eat small rodents, birds, and young rabbits.

WHERE IT LIVES

Bullsnakes are found on the Great Plains.

A kind of bullsnake known as the gopher snake is found in the western United States.

A type of bullsnake known as the pine snake is found in the eastern United States.

12

SPECIAL WARNING

Bullsnakes will strike if bothered. Don't get too close!

CORN SNAKE

Tips to find this snake

The corn snake is active at night.

It likes barns and ditches where it can find food and shelter.

It hides during the day in gopher burrows or under logs or rocks.

WHAT IT LOOKS LIKE

The corn snake's body is yellow-brown to gray. It has red-brown saddle-shaped blotches along its back and sides. Its belly has black bars or checker-shapes on it.

Its sturdy and solid body can grow to be 2 to 4 feet long.

WHAT IT EATS

Corn snakes eat small animals such as mice, birds, and rabbits.

WHERE IT LIVES

Corn snakes can be found from New Jersey south to Florida, west to Nebraska and New Mexico.

INTERESTING FACTS

This snake got its name by often being found in corn fields.

Don't approach or touch any wild animals you might see.

RAT SNAKE

Tips to find this snake

Rat snakes like woods, rocky hillsides and farmyards.

In spring and fall, the snake is active during the day.

In summer it is active at night.

It may be found in barns and stables where it looks for mice and rats to eat.

WHAT IT LOOKS LIKE

Some rat snakes have solid black bodies. Some have red, yellow or gray bodies with 4 dark stripes from head to tail. Others have a tannish body with dark blotches. All rat snakes have tan bellies.

Rat snakes have thick, sturdy bodies and grow to be 3 to 6 feet long.

WHAT IT EATS

Rat snakes eat frogs, mice, small rabbits, and lizards.

WHERE IT LIVES

They are found from Maine south along the east coast into Florida, also west to Texas and north to Iowa.

SPECIAL WARNING

They bite if threatened.

MAKE A DRIED BEAN PICTURE

WHAT YOU NEED

- piece of posterboard about 12 x 18 inches large

- fine-point marker

- bottle of glue

- dried beans and peas: kidney beans are red, black beans are black, split peas are green, navy beans are white, lentils are yellow, and pinto beans spotted.

- newspaper

- damp washcloth

- masking tape for hanging

WHAT TO DO

1 Spread the newspaper over your workspace.

2 Divide up the beans and peas, putting each color in a pile.

3 Use this book to choose a snake, a salamander, or a lizard.

4 With the marker, draw the outline of the animal onto the posterboard.

5 Draw its bands or blotches or spots of color.

6 Spread glue on one of the spots or blotches, using your fingers.

7 Wipe your fingers clean with the damp washcloth.

8 Carefully place the beans with colors matching the picture onto the glue.

9 Make sure to put the beans close together.

10 Repeat with the other sections, making sure to use the right colors.

11 Let the finished picture dry, then hang it on your wall or door.

15

SALAMANDERS

Salamanders are animals known as amphibians. Amphibians have smooth skin. They can live on land and in the water.

Salamanders are most abundant in North America. The United States alone has 135 kinds.

They have long tails and long bodies.

Most salamanders have 4 legs. Others have only 2 legs. Some have no legs.

Most are active at night.

They have 4 toes on each front foot.

Most salamanders have 5 toes on each hind foot. The toes do not have claws.

All salamanders avoid the sun.

They can repair almost any injury to their bodies.

They can regrow new tails, legs, and feet.

Be kind to all animals.

MUDPUPPY

Tips to find this salamander

Mudpuppies live only in cool, fresh water, like streams.

At night, look in the streambed while they are feeding.

During the day, they hide under rocks in the stream.

Mudpuppies are active all year, even in winter.

WHAT IT LOOKS LIKE

A mudpuppy has a grayish to dark brown smooth body. It has 3 red, frilly gills on each side of the head.

Mudpuppies can grow to be 15 inches long. They have 4 short legs.

WHAT IT EATS

Mudpuppies eat crayfish, insects, worms, and fish.

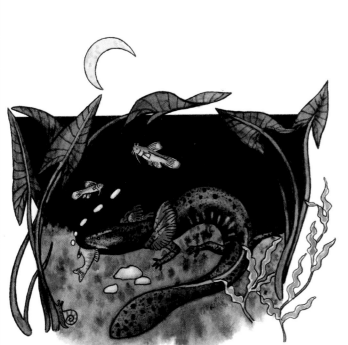

WHERE IT LIVES

Mudpuppies live throughout the north-eastern United States, and through the Great Lakes down to Kansas and southern Missouri.

Use the ruler on the back of this book to measure what you find.

SIREN

Tips to find this salamander

Sirens live in warm, still water such as ditches and swamps.

Sirens are most active at night.

They hide during the day under rocks and logs, and among water plants.

WHAT IT LOOKS LIKE

The siren's slender dark gray-brown body has black spots. It has 3 pairs of blue-gray gills just behind the head.

A siren looks like an eel. Its body grows from 6 inches long to as much as 50 inches. It has 2 tiny front feet, but no back feet.

WHAT IT EATS

Sirens eat crayfish, worms, clams, and some water plants.

WHERE IT LIVES

Sirens are found along the coastal southeastern United States from South Carolina and Florida, west to Texas and up the Mississippi River valley.

Pay attention to everything around you.

TIGER SALAMANDER

Tips to find this salamander

Tiger salamanders live in grassy or swampy burrows.

In spring, they travel at night to shallow ponds.

During rainy times, look for them under rocks or logs. They may even lie in window wells or wander across roads.

Interesting Facts

Tiger salamanders are the largest land salamanders in the world.

Some young tiger salamanders eat each other! Maybe it is their big appetite that gives them their name.

WHAT IT LOOKS LIKE

The tiger salamander has smooth, dark-brown or black skin. It has white, gold, or greenish spots and blotches on top. Underneath, its belly is green-yellow. The body is thick, and the head is wide.

A tiger salamander grows to be 13 inches long. It has 4 short, stout legs.

WHAT IT EATS

Tiger salamanders always seem to be hungry.

They like worms, mice, and insects such as crickets.

WHERE IT LIVES

Tiger salamanders are found across the United States, but they are rare in the Appalachian mountains, the north-eastern and Pacific states.

Wear boots, gloves and long pants.

SPOTTED SALAMANDER

Spotted salamanders often live in underground burrows made by other animals, such as moles or rats.

Tips to find this salamander

Spotted salamanders like quiet forests with ponds.

Spotted salamanders are active at night, especially along pond edges in late winter.

WHAT IT LOOKS LIKE

The spotted salamander has a black or dark brown body. It has an uneven row of yellow or orange spots along each side of its body (but none on the belly). The belly is gray-blue and lightly speckled. Its body is thick, with shallow dents along its body.

Spotted salamanders are usually 6 to 10 inches long. They have 4 chubby legs.

WHAT IT EATS

Spotted salamanders eat insects, earthworms, snails, and spiders.

WHERE IT LIVES

Spotted salamanders live in the eastern United States as far west as the Texas/Oklahoma border, and north to the Great Lakes region.

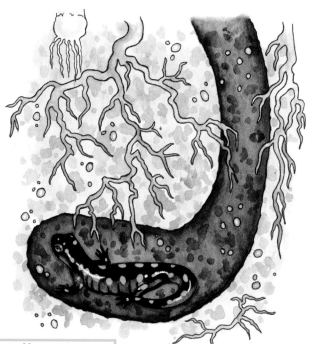

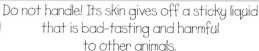

SPECIAL WARNING

Do not handle! Its skin gives off a sticky liquid that is bad-tasting and harmful to other animals.

RED EFT

Tips to find this salamander

Red efts are easiest to find in September and October, just before the winter frost. At this time, young red efts leave the ponds for their years on land. Look under rocks and logs in woods for them.

Also in September and October, mature red efts head to freshwater ponds. Their skin color changes from red-orange to green-brown.

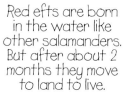

Red efts are born in the water like other salamanders. But after about 2 months they move to land to live.

After 2 to 3 years the adult is now called a red-spotted newt. It then moves back into the water to live.

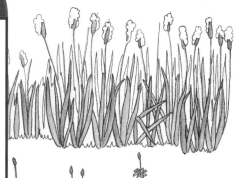

WHAT IT LOOKS LIKE

Red efts have red-orange bodies. There are a few small red spots on its back and sides. Its skin is rough and dry, not slimy.

The red eft grows to be 1-1/2 inches to 3-1/2 inches long, and is slender in shape with a worm-like tail. It has 4 short, slender legs.

WHAT IT EATS

Red efts eat small worms and insects such as flies.

WHERE IT LIVES

Red efts are found east of the Mississippi River.

SPECIAL WARNING

Do not touch! Your mouth and eyes will sting and burn if you touch them after touching a red eft.

FOUR-TOED SALAMANDER

INTERESTING FACTS

Its name comes from having only 4 toes on each hind foot. (Most salamanders have 5.)

When it is threatened, the four-toed salamander waves its tail in the air to scare the enemy.

Tips to find this salamander

Four-toed salamanders are active at night.

They like wet and muddy ground where moss covers rotting logs.

Four-toed salamanders hide in moss in late summer.

WHAT IT LOOKS LIKE

The four-toed salamander has red-brown skin that looks speckled along its gray sides. Its white belly looks as if it is sprinkled with pepper.

The body is slender and grows to be 2-1/2 to 4 inches long. Four-toed salamanders have 4 short, slender legs.

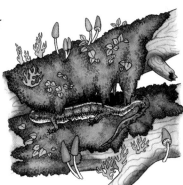

WHAT IT EATS

It eats small spiders, insects, and worms.

WHERE IT LIVES

Four-toed salamanders live east of the Mississippi River.

Wear boots! Take a flashlight. Carefully peel back the moss while you are searching. Always put back any moss you disturb.

TWO-LINED SALAMANDER

Tips to find this salamander

Look along the edges of small streams and creeks.

It is active at night when it looks for food.

Sometimes, it climbs short plants to find food.

Two-lined salamanders eat small water insects and snails.

WHERE IT LIVES

Two-lined salamanders live in the Appalachian Mountains of the southeastern United States.

INTERESTING FACTS

This animal is nicknamed the "brookside salamander" because it lives beside small streams, called brooks.

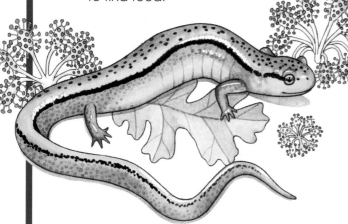

WHAT IT LOOKS LIKE

The two-lined salamander is tan, with black stripes on the top of each side. It has a slender and narrow body.

It grows to be 2 to 4 inches long. It has a long tail and 4 short, skinny legs.

Take a drawing pad and a pencil when you go exploring.

MARBLED SALAMANDER

Tips to find this salamander

Look in dry woods beneath
leaf piles and logs,
and in burrows.

During summer and autumn,
marbled salamanders
guard the eggs they have
laid in dried-up ponds.

WHAT IT LOOKS LIKE

Marbled salamanders have dark brown to
black bellies. Their bodies are white along
the top, with chocolate brown blotches.

Its body is pudgy and grows to be about 5
inches long. It has 4 thick, short legs.

INTERESTING FACTS

Marbled
salamander adults
can't swim but
their babies
live in water.

WHAT IT EATS

Marbled salamanders eat
grubs and insects
such as spiders.

WHERE IT LIVES

Marbled salamanders live
from Florida west to Texas
along the Gulf Coast,
and north to the Great Lakes
and the New England states.

Don't leave behind any litter.

TWO-LINED SALAMANDER

Tips to find this salamander

Look along the edges of small streams and creeks.

It is active at night when it looks for food.

Sometimes, it climbs short plants to find food.

WHAT IT EATS

Two-lined salamanders eat small water insects and snails.

WHERE IT LIVES

Two-lined salamanders live in the Appalachian Mountains of the southeastern United States.

INTERESTING FACTS

This animal is nicknamed the "brookside salamander" because it lives beside small streams, called brooks.

WHAT IT LOOKS LIKE

The two-lined salamander is tan, with black stripes on the top of each side. It has a slender and narrow body.

It grows to be 2 to 4 inches long. It has a long tail and 4 short, skinny legs.

Take a drawing pad and a pencil when you go exploring.

SLIMY SALAMANDER

Tips to find this salamander

Slimy salamanders like cool, moist areas such as rocky banks or caves.

They can also be found under flat rocks or logs.

They come out at night to feed.

They are especially active in wet weather.

WHAT IT LOOKS LIKE

Slimy salamanders have blue-black skin with white speckles. They have thin, smooth bodies.

They grow to be about 7 inches long with 4 short, skinny legs.

WHAT IT EATS

Slimy salamanders eat ants, beetles, earthworms, and slugs.

WHERE IT LIVES

Slimy salamanders live from New England south to the Gulf Coast, southwest to Oklahoma, and into central Texas.

Always bring drinking water with you.

LONGTAIL SALAMANDER

Tips to find this salamander

They like moist, sheltered places like cracks between rocks.

Look in rocky banks and under rocks near ponds and streams.

They hide during the day and come out in early evening to eat.

Sometimes they climb logs and tree trunks looking for food.

WHAT IT LOOKS LIKE

The longtail salamander's skin is yellow-orange with dark brown or black spots. The spots form Vs on the long tail. Its belly is yellow and usually not spotted.

Longtail salamanders can grow to be 6 inches long. They have thin bodies with 4 short, skinny legs.

WHAT IT EATS

They eat small insects such as spiders and worms.

WHERE IT LIVES

Longtail salamanders live from southern New York state to northern Alabama, and from the Atlantic coast west to Missouri.

INTERESTING FACTS

The longtail salamander gets its name from its very long tail.

SPECIAL NOTE

Take a flashlight! The light will not bother this salamander, so you can watch it. Wear boots—you might be in wet places.

Watch where you step.

MARBLED SALAMANDER

Tips to find this salamander

Look in dry woods beneath
leaf piles and logs,
and in burrows.

During summer and autumn,
marbled salamanders
guard the eggs they have
laid in dried-up ponds.

WHAT IT LOOKS LIKE

Marbled salamanders have dark brown to
black bellies. Their bodies are white along
the top, with chocolate brown blotches.

Its body is pudgy and grows to be about 5
inches long. It has 4 thick, short legs.

Interesting Facts

Marbled
salamander adults
can't swim but
their babies
live in water.

WHAT IT EATS

Marbled salamanders eat
grubs and insects
such as spiders.

WHERE IT LIVES

Marbled salamanders live
from Florida west to Texas
along the Gulf Coast,
and north to the Great Lakes
and the New England states.

Don't leave behind any litter.

MAKE A "STAINED GLASS" ANIMAL

WHAT YOU NEED

- newspaper

- bottle of glue

- black construction paper

- scissors

- tissue paper in different colors

- masking tape for hanging

- white crayon

WHAT TO DO

1 Spread the newspaper over your work area.

2 Use this book to choose a salamander, a snake, or a lizard with bright spots or blotches.

3 Draw the outline of the animal you choose onto the black construction paper, using the white crayon. Also draw its spots or blotches. You can make the animal larger on the paper than it really is.

4 Using the scissors, cut along the outline.

5 Then, cut out each of the spots and blotches with the scissors, so the animal outline looks "holey."

6 Next, cut out bigger shapes from the colored tissue paper.

7 Put glue around the edge of each hole and stick a piece of tissue in place on the back side of the outline.

8 Let the glue dry.

9 Using the masking tape, tape your "stained glass" animal to a window where the light can shine through the tissue paper.

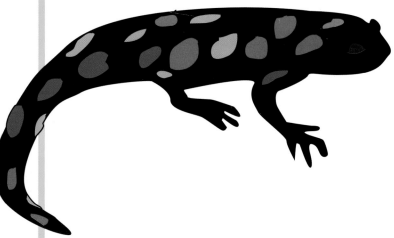

27

LIZARDS

Lizards, like snakes, are animals known as reptiles.

There are about 90 kinds of lizards in the United States.

Lizards have long bodies and long tails.

They usually have 4 legs. Others have 2 legs. Some lizards have no legs.

Usually, lizards have 5 toes on each front foot.

The toes have claws.

Lizard skin is dry. It is covered with scales.

Some lizards are very fast, and can run up to 15 miles per hour!

Most can also swim.

If their tail is broken off, they can grow a new one.

Don't hurry. Take your time and have fun!

SKINK

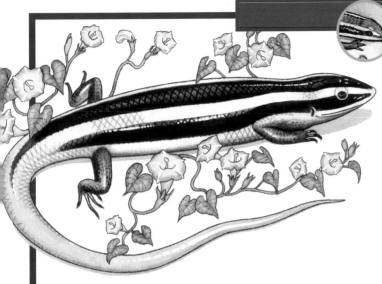

WHAT IT LOOKS LIKE

Some skinks have a solid body color. Others have lines that run the length of the body. Smooth, flat scales give its body a glossy shine.

Skinks grow to be about 12 inches long. Some look like a snake or worm with very short legs.

WHAT IT EATS

Most skinks eat grubs and insects such as ants and worms.

Some skinks also eat plants.

WHERE IT LIVES

Skinks can be found all over the United States, except for the high western mountains.

Interesting Facts

Skinks have scales with little pieces of bone in them, so all together they are like a suit of armor.

Some skinks have no legs and burrow underground.

Tips to find this lizard

Skinks like undisturbed places, such as rock piles and vacant lots.

Look for them from spring through fall only. They hibernate in the winter.

They are active during the day, especially when it is warm.

Tell an adult how long you will be gone.

FENCE LIZARD

Tips to find this lizard

Fence lizards like quiet places, such as rock piles and fences around pastures.

They also live in trees and shrubs.

They are active during the day.

WHAT IT LOOKS LIKE

Fence lizards are gray or brown. Some have uneven black Vs on their back and tail. Males have at least 1 blue patch on the throat.

Fence lizards grow to be 3 to 8 inches long. They have slender bodies and long tails.

WHAT IT EATS

Fence lizards eat insects such as spiders.

WHERE IT LIVES

Fence lizards live from Delaware south to Florida and west to Arizona.

INTERESTING FACTS

Fence lizards are nicknamed "swifts" because they are hard to catch.

Lift rocks away from you when exploring.

BANDED GECKO

Tips to find this lizard

Banded geckos are active at night from June through September. They hibernate during other months.

They like rocky sand deserts.

They hide during the day under rocks, boards, or litter.

WHAT IT LOOKS LIKE

A banded gecko has a cream-colored body with brown blotches across its back and sides. The skin is soft. Its body is covered with fine scales that look like beads.

Banded geckos grow to be about 6 inches long. They have thin bodies with long tails.

WHAT IT EATS

Banded geckos eat small insects such as spiders.

WHERE IT LIVES

Geckos live in the southwestern deserts and canyons, from California east to Texas.

Don't approach or touch any wild plants you don't know. Stay away from poison ivy and poison oak.

GREEN ANOLE

Tips to find this lizard

It is active during the day.

Anoles climb trees, shrubs, fences, and also walls of old buildings.

They like shady places when it is hot.

SPECIAL NOTE
Look for this animal during or after a rain. The green anole gets all of its water from droplets it licks off places like leaves or posts.

INTERESTING FACTS

The green anole can change its body color from green to brown in just minutes.

Anoles have sticky toe pads and thumblike toes that help them grab and hold as they climb.

WHAT IT LOOKS LIKE

Green anoles vary in color from bright green to dark brown. Males have a pink flap of skin on the throat.

The anole grows to be about 5 to 8 inches long and has a thin body. Its head has a narrow snout.

WHAT IT EATS

Anoles eat insects such as cockroaches, crickets, and flies.

WHERE IT LIVES

Anoles live from southern Virginia south to Florida, and west to Texas and Oklahoma.

SPECIAL WARNING
Anoles like to jump— don't be surprised when they do!

COLLARED LIZARD

Tips to find this lizard

Collared lizards are active during the day.

They like dry rock piles and gullies.

Look for them on sunny days, resting on rocks.

WHAT IT LOOKS LIKE

The collared lizard has a lime green body with brown stripes across its back. Collared lizards have large heads.

It grows to be about 12 inches long with a heavy, solid body and a long skinny tail.

WHAT IT EATS

Collared lizards eat small lizards and large insects like grasshoppers.

WHERE IT LIVES

Collared lizards live west of the Mississippi River and less commonly in the southeastern states.

INTERESTING FACTS

This lizard is named for the 2 black rings that look like a collar around its neck.

The collared lizard stands up and runs on its back legs.

SPECIAL WARNING

They will bite if you try to touch them. Be careful!

33

SIDE-BLOTCHED LIZARD

Tips to find this lizard

Side-blotched lizards like rocky places.

They use packrat burrows to escape the desert midday heat.

They are active in cool morning hours and in the late afternoon.

In the spring, males perch on large rocks and watch for other males that might trespass in their territory.

WHAT IT LOOKS LIKE

The side blotched lizard's skin is tannish-brown with light-colored spots. The slender body is covered with fine, overlapping scales.

Side-blotched lizards grow to be about 6 inches long.

WHAT IT EATS

Side-blotched lizards eat small insects such as black ants, beetles, locusts, and flies.

They even eat scorpions!

INTERESTING FACTS

Their name comes from the blotch of blue or black behind each front leg.

WHERE IT LIVES

Side-blotched lizards are found from California and Arizona into Utah and northwest to Washington. They also live in New Mexico and Texas.

Don't put your hand into any holes or burrows or cracks. They may be animals' homes.

LEOPARD LIZARD

Tips to find this lizard

Leopard lizards like dry, open, flat ground.

On hot days, look for them in the shade of a plant.

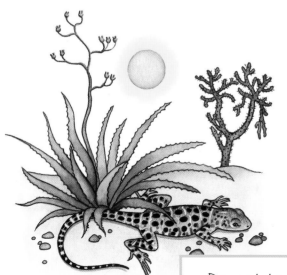

WHAT IT LOOKS LIKE

Leopard lizards have black blotches and small red patches over a brown body. Their bellies are light brown or gray.

They grow to be about 8 to 15 inches long and are slender.

INTERESTING FACTS

The leopard lizard gets its name from the many spots on its body.

WHAT IT EATS

Leopard lizards eat large insects such as grasshoppers, and smaller lizards (even other leopard lizards).

They also eat berries.

WHERE IT LIVES

Leopard lizards live in the desert areas of southern Oregon and Idaho, south into California and southeast to Texas.

Do not touch—they will bite!

SPECIAL WARNING

HORNED LIZARD

Tips to find this lizard

It is active only during the day.

Horned lizards are hard to see. Their blotchy skin helps them blend in.

Look on rocks, where they wait for prey to pass by.

Sometimes, they lie half-buried in the sand or under a cactus.

They like flat, sandy, open areas.

SPECIAL NOTE

If startled, the horned lizard may run a short ways and then freeze, blending in again.

When threatened, it may spray blood from the corners of its eyes at its enemy.

INTERESTING FACTS

The horned lizard uses its sticky tongue to pick up poisonous ants without harming itself.

It gets its name from the "horns" across the top of its head.

It looks like a small dinosaur!

WHAT IT LOOKS LIKE

The blotchy brown-and-tan skin has spines on the head and also along the sides of the body. The body is rounded with a short tail. The muscular legs and clawed feet are used for digging.

Horned lizards grow to be about 4 inches long.

WHAT IT EATS

Ants, crickets, sow bugs, and other small insects are food for the horned lizard.

WHERE IT LIVES

Horned lizards live in desert areas of the western and southwestern United States (including Texas) and north to Kansas.

SPECIAL WARNING

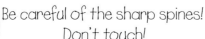

Be careful of the sharp spines! Don't touch!

GILA MONSTER

WHAT IT LOOKS LIKE

The gila monster has a dark brown body with pale orange blotches. The belly is black. The skin looks beaded. Its body is broad, and it has a long tail.

The gila monster is big! It grows to be 1 to 2 feet long.

WHAT IT EATS

The gila monster eats small birds, mice, insects, and eggs. It also eats dead animals.

WHERE IT LIVES

Gila monsters live in Nevada, Arizona, California, Utah, Texas, and New Mexico.

Tips to find this lizard

Gila monsters like rocky deserts, canyons near water, and scrubby forests.

Sometimes they climb trees looking for food.

Gila monsters are most active at dawn or dusk.

They hide under large rocks during the heat of the day.

Don't touch! Don't get too close.

Venom is released as the Gila monster bites and chews. The bite can be fatal to dogs and harmful to you.

Gila monsters have a strong grip. If provoked, they will grab on and not let go!

SPECIAL WARNING

INTERESTING FACTS

The gila monster is the only lizard in the United States that is poisonous.

The gila monster smells with its tongue!

Gila monsters sleep on their backs with their legs sprawled out.

CHUCKWALLA

Tips to find this lizard

Chuckwallas live in large rock slabs, like blocks of lava, where there are many cracks.

They are active during the day.

WHAT IT LOOKS LIKE

The chuckwalla's yellowish skin looks mud-splattered. It has loose skin along the neck and body. It has a flat body with a long skinny tail.

The chuckwalla is a big lizard. It can grow to be 1 to 2 feet long.

WHAT IT EATS

Chuckwallas eat the buds, flowers and leaves of plants.

WHERE IT LIVES

Chuckwallas live in southern California, north into Nevada, Utah, and Arizona.

Wear a hat and use sunscreen to protect yourself from the sun.

MAKE A CLAY MODEL

WHAT YOU NEED

- a flat surface, such as a table, that will not be damaged by clay

- Popsicle stick

- fork

- stick of modeling clay

- plastic bag

- damp washcloth

WHAT TO DO

1 On the flat surface, shape the clay into your favorite animals from this book. Snakes can be made by rolling clay into a long rope.

2 Use the Popsicle stick and the fork to add details to the animal's "skin," like a scaly pattern, lines, or bumps. The fork can be used to add eyes and toes.

3 The animals can be shown sleeping or hunting. You can change the shape or the position many times.

4 When you are finished playing, store the clay in the plastic bag.

5 Clean up the surface and your hands with the washcloth.

6 If you have the kind of clay that gets hard, you can let your animal dry and keep it forever.

For More Information

MORE BOOKS TO READ

Chameleons: Masters of Disguise. Secrets of the Animal World series. Eulalia García (Gareth Stevens)

FANGS! series. Eric Ethan (Gareth Stevens)

Reptiles. Wonderful World of Animals series. Beatrice MacLeod (Gareth Stevens)

Salamanders. Cherie Winner (Lerner Group)

The World of Reptiles. Darlyne Murawski (Newbridge Communications)

VIDEOS

Reptiles Are Interesting. (Phoenix/BFA Films and Video)
Snakes. (Rainbow Educational Video)
Snakes and the Like. (Agency for Instructional Technology)

WEB SITES

www.olcommerce.com/terra/reptile.html
//members.aol.com/iguanabeme/home.html

INDEX